D1358032

Animal Builders

A Bird's Nest

Niles Worthington

Cavendish
Square

New York

Published in 2017 by Cavendish Square Publishing, LLC
243 5th Avenue, Suite 136, New York, NY 10016

Copyright © 2017 by Cavendish Square Publishing, LLC

First Edition

Library of Congress Cataloging-in-Publication Data

Names: Worthington, Niles.
Title: A bird's nest / Niles Worthington.
Description: New York : Cavendish Square, 2017. | Series: Animal builders | Includes index.
Identifiers: ISBN 9781502622655 (pbk.) | ISBN 9781502620804 (library bound) | ISBN 9781502620798 (6 pack) | ISBN 9781502620811 (ebook)
Subjects: LCSH: Birds--Nests--Juvenile literature. | Birds--Juvenile literature.
Classification: LCC QL675.W67 2017 | DDC 598.156'4--dc23

Editorial Director: David McNamara
Editor: Fletcher Doyle
Copy Editor: Rebecca Rohan
Assistant Art Director: Amy Greenan
Designer: Stephanie Flecha
Production Coordinator: Karol Szymczuk
Photo Research: J8 Media

Printed in the United States of America

Contents

Birds lay eggs in nests. Baby **chicks** hatch from the eggs. Birds feed chicks in nests.

Eagles build big nests.
They put them up high.

Birds hang nests for safety.
They **weave** nests with grass.

Barn swallows build on walls.
They use mud.

Woodpeckers nest in trees.
Chicks sleep on wood chips.

13

Burrowing birds dig nests. They dig in soft dirt.

15

Birds build with string.
They find what you drop.

17

Birds line nests with pet fur.
It warms the chicks.

19

Birds **hide** nests in trees.
You can see them after
the leaves fall.

21

New Words

burrowing (BIR-owe-ing) Making a hole or tunnel to live in.

chicks (CHIX) Birds that have just hatched.

hide (HYDE) Put a thing out of sight.

line (LYN) To cover the inside surface.

weave (WEEV) To form by lacing parts together.

Index

23

About the Author

Niles Worthington plays soccer and tennis and enjoys writing children's books. He works as a pharmacist and loves studying nature.

About BOOKWORMS

Bookworms help independent readers gain reading confidence through high-frequency words, simple sentences, and strong picture/text support. Each book explores a concept that helps children relate what they read to the world they live in.